Columbus Museum of Art

The Essential Thread
Tapestry on Wall and Body

Lotus Stack

The Minneapolis Institute of Arts

This book was produced in conjunction with the exhibition "The Essential Thread: Tapestry on Wall and Body," held at The Minneapolis Institute of Arts, 25 June–2 October 1988.

Designed by Anne Knauff
Edited by Elisabeth Sövik
Photographs by Gary Mortensen
Line drawings by Abby Sue Fisher

©1988 by The Minneapolis Institute of Arts
2400 Third Avenue South
Minneapolis, Minnesota 55404
All rights reserved
Printed in the United States of America

Library of Congress Catalog Card Number 88-60727
International Standard Book Number 0-912964-36-7

This publication was funded in part by the Andrew W. Mellon Foundation and by a grant from the National Endowment for the Arts, a federal agency.

Cover illustration:
Queen Esther and King Ahasuerus, detail
Flanders, mid-15th century
Wool and silk
Gift of Mrs. C. J. Martin for the Charles Jairus Martin Memorial Collection   16.721

NK 2985 .M5 A4 1988x

Stack, Lotus.

The Essential thread

Contents

Preface	4
Introduction	5
Egypt	6
The Middle East	8
India	12
China and Japan	16
The Americas	20
Europe	24
Tapestry Techniques	30
Appendix	36
Suggested Reading	37
Exhibition Staff	38

Preface

This is the second in a series of books on the textile collection of The Minneapolis Institute of Arts. Each one presents a technique of cloth making and discusses its use by various cultures throughout history. Besides introducing the museum's textile holdings, these publications provide general information that will help readers appreciate other textiles they may encounter.

The Essential Thread explains how tapestry cloth is woven and describes various fabrics with this distinctive structure. It is not a complete survey of all tapestry-woven cloth, but covers tapestry production only in those geographical areas where pieces in the museum's collection originated. Thus, it does not deal with tapestry from Africa, Indonesia, or the Philippines. For readers interested in pursuing the topic further, a brief bibliography is included. A summary of the museum's tapestry holdings appears in the Appendix.

My initial consideration of technical and historical concepts was broadened and refined through discussions with a number of artists, weavers, and textile historians. I am especially grateful to Archie Brennan, Jim Brown, Sheila Hicks, Jean Pierre Larochette, Hal Painter, Ruth Scheuer, Adolph Cavallo, and Noboku Kajitani for their many helpful comments and suggestions.

For their efforts in the preparation of this catalogue and exhibition I extend special thanks to Mary Ann Butterfield, Peggy Dorwick, and Barbara Tennis, of the Textile Department staff; editor Elisabeth Sövik; designers Roxy Ballard and Anne Knauff; Gwen Bitz, the museum's registrar, and Karen Duncan, associate registrar; Gary Mortensen and Robert Fogt, photographers; Patrick Atherton, typesetter; John Black, lighting technician; and Tom Jance, Patti Landres, Doug Kroeger, Wayne Masterson, Charley Foster, and Brian Stieler, exhibition technicians. Michael Conforti and Timothy Fiske, interim co-directors, have supported this project with enthusiasm. Funding for the exhibition and catalogue was organized by Beth Desnick and Loren Niemi. Mark Stanley and James Ockuly, of the museum's media department, produced the video complement to the exhibition. I especially appreciate Edward Stack's continuing support throughout the catalogue writing and exhibition development. Finally, I wish to express my gratitude to Roberta and Richard Simmons, Carol Ann MacKay, John Bryns, Mary Pawlcyn, Lydia Kulesov, and Mary Temple, whose generous loans have enhanced the exhibition immeasurably.

Introduction

Today, we tend to take cloth for granted, but this is a fairly new attitude. Until the nineteenth century, all fabric was made by hand from fibers laboriously gathered from the land or obtained from animals. Next to agriculture, textile production was the most labor-intensive activity of humankind.

Cloth production undoubtedly developed to meet very basic physical needs, but it satisfied aesthetic needs as well. As weaving technology developed, weavers devised many different textile structures appropriate for the purposes their cloth would serve.

The term tapestry is often associated with the large pictorial wall hangings of medieval and Renaissance Europe. In fact, however, tapestry is a distinctive woven structure in which the design is integral to the cloth and appears more or less the same on both sides of the fabric. The tapestry structure is well suited to complex patterning, yet it can be woven on even the most elementary loom. It can be used for fabrics ranging from heavy, durable floor coverings, such as the Middle Eastern kilim, to delicate garments like the Kashmir shawl or Chinese silks.

Weavers all over the world have used the tapestry structure to create magnificent textiles. The kings and aristocracy of Europe commissioned large wall hangings for their cold castles. Chinese emperors established imperial workshops where weavers made religious vestments, throne cushions, banners, wall hangings, and court robes. Roman senators, Persian and Indian nobles, Syrian sherifs, Inca emperors, Navajo chiefs, and Mexican caballeros all wore clothing embellished with this form of weaving.

The weavers who made these remarkable textiles were highly skilled. Much of the European, Egyptian, Indian, and Chinese tapestry-woven cloth was made in well-organized workshops with an extremely specialized division of labor, and working conditions were often controlled by government or guild regulations. But fine tapestry fabric was also made under other conditions. Wonderful blankets, carrying bags, and floor coverings have been woven by women working in their homes in remote parts of the American Southwest or in the rural areas of the Middle East.

Tapestry weaving can be very slow. Sometimes it takes years to finish a single piece. Fine tapestry fabrics have always been very costly to make, so usually only the rich and powerful were able to own them. Even today tapestry is made by hand because mechanizing the process by which it is woven has never been economically practical.

With the advent of the industrial age in the late eighteenth century, Western consumers began to favor patterned fabrics that could be produced on power looms, and the popularity of tapestry-woven cloth waned. But in the late nineteenth century, the Arts and Crafts movement, initiated by the famous English designer William Morris, revitalized tapestry weaving in England and Scandinavia. And in the twentieth century, the artist Jean Lurçat infused new life into French tapestry design. In the United States, a few workshops have produced European-style pictorial wall hangings. Today several small workshops and a considerable number of independent artists around the world are creating tapestry-woven hangings. Although the domestic needs that formerly motivated rural weavers are now filled by industrially woven cloth, a renewed interest in handwoven cloth and in ethnic culture has developed a new market, and thus tapestry weaving continues in various parts of Mexico, the American Southwest, and the Middle East.

Egypt

The oldest known pieces of tapestry-woven fabric come from Egypt. Textiles found in ancient tombs indicate that tapestry weaving was carried on there over three thousand years ago. Whether the technique actually originated in Egypt is not known, but the climate and social customs were conducive to the preservation of textiles. The Egyptians interred textiles and other household objects with their dead, and the dryness of the desert tombs helped to preserve many of those items. But though the earliest tapestry remains date from pharaonic times, it was not until the beginning of the Christian era that Egyptian weavers fully developed tapestry as an art form.

Weaving materials were readily available. For centuries Egypt had been the leading exporter of flax and linen cloth to the ancient Mediterranean world. Flax fiber was so widely used throughout the Roman Empire that when the emperor Gallienus, in the third century A.D., learned of a revolt in Egypt, he exclaimed, "What! Can we get along without Egyptian flax?" Though not as common as flax, wool was also produced in Egypt and exported. Roman army supply records from the Judaean and the Cappadocian commands include orders for woolen garments to be made in Egypt. Through the eastern trade, silk, too, could be had, but it was expensive and used only in luxury fabrics.

The importance of textile production in Roman Egypt is attested by census records and tax and trade reports. Although domestic cloth and clothing were occasionally made in the home, for the most part weaving was a professional occupation, and even a poor person normally bought ready-made clothing. Production and costs were closely controlled by government and guild. In small towns and even in the larger urban centers, workshops were generally quite small, averaging two to four looms. A workshop might be attached to a house and run primarily by family members, or work space could be leased. There were a number of state-supported factories and also a few temple workshops, but they were much smaller than in pharaonic times and eventually disappeared altogether.

Weavers were ranked from apprentice to master, and workshops employed both freemen and slaves. Payment was either by the piece or a fixed wage. At the beginning of the Christian era many weavers, especially those producing luxury goods, earned a decent living. But the fall of the western Roman Empire in the fifth century and the Arab Muslim invasions of the seventh brought changes that left Egyptian weavers in dire economic straits.

Raw materials such as wool and flax were usually bought already processed from the spinners or yarn merchants. There are no records of spinning guilds, so it seems likely that spinning was done mainly by women in their spare time, as it is today in some parts of the Middle East and North Africa. Dyeing was a separate trade and the dyers had their own guilds.

From the beginning of the third century through the end of the twelfth, tapestry was popular as a technique for decorating clothing and other textiles. Native Egyptian weavers, many of whom were Coptic Christians, explored the subtleties possible with this structure and created everything from elaborate fringes to intricate hangings depicting figural as well as floral and geometric motifs.

Weavers commonly worked on a horizontal loom prepared with a linen warp. Most of the pattern was executed with a wool weft, with linen and sometimes silk used for shading and special effects. Slit tapestry was the favored technique, but warp interlocks were also employed when needed for structural stability. The weft was generally kept perpendicular to the warp; however, eccentric wefts were often used to emphasize curvilinear forms, and this was accomplished so skillfully that it rarely caused surface distortion.

Most weaving was done on commission, whether in large quantities for the government or as single pieces for an individual customer. The cost depended on the fineness of the fabric and the intricacy of the design; fine fabrics could be twenty times more expensive than the coarsest ones. The fineness of the cloth thus reflected the customer's wealth.

During the first centuries of the Christian era, the shape and placement of the decoration on a garment often indicated the political rank and thus the social standing of the wearer. Pagan motifs and images of the Roman gods were initially favored, but as the influence of Christianity became more pervasive the popularity and significance of pagan imagery diminished. Some motifs were reinterpreted in Christian terms; for

Sanctuary curtain
6th century
Inset tapestry patterning
Linen and wool
Gift of the Aimee Mott Butler Charitable Trust, Mr. and Mrs. John F. Donovan, the estate of Margaret B. Hawks, and Eleanor Weld Reid   83.126

example, the grape leaf, which had referred to the Roman god Bacchus, later came to be associated with Christ.

In the middle of the seventh century, when Arab Muslims conquered Egypt and Islam became the dominant political and religious force, the intricate geometric designs so typical of Islamic art began to appear in Egyptian textiles. Most of the weavers, however, were Christians and continued to use some figural imagery.

As in ancient Egyptian weaving, ornamental tapestry work was frequently inset into the cloth during the weaving process, with the weaver making the necessary technical adjustments. Such fabric was often made into clothing, and the ornamentation was woven in place according to the type of garment intended. Sometimes tapestry roundels and squares were woven separately and then appliquéd to a finished garment.

Large hangings were among the outstanding achievements of the Egyptian tapestry weavers. The Coptic sanctuary curtain owned by The Minneapolis Institute of Arts, with its large Latin cross, is particularly rare. Not only is such overt Christian imagery unusual, but when crosses are depicted they are generally of the Greek (equal-armed) type. Although lighter in weight and from a different artistic heritage, these hangings directly influenced the French and Flemish tapestry wall coverings so popular in Europe from the Middle Ages up until the nineteenth century.

For centuries Egyptian fabrics were a prized item in many parts of the world. During the period of Roman occupation, textiles were regularly shipped by sea from Alexandria east to Yemen and India and west to Italy and Spain. Yet because few places in the world are as conducive to the preservation of textiles as Egypt, few examples of Egyptian weaving have survived elsewhere. However, early in this century several tapestry-woven fragments dating from the fifth to seventh centuries were discovered by the British archaeologist Aurel Stein in the Takla Makan desert in northwestern China. And so it may be that the influence of the Egyptian tapestry weavers was even more extensive than previously thought.

Opposite: *Kilim*
Turkey, 19th century
Wool
Gift of Miss Lily Place   31.81.7

Below: detail

The Middle East

The Middle East is one of the few areas of the world where tapestry has not been exclusively a luxury fabric for the urban elite. Luxury woven goods were produced in towns and cities, but the semi-nomadic tribes of the region used the tapestry structure to create sturdy, decorative household fabrics.

The Nomadic Tradition

Probably the most familiar tapestry item of the Middle East is the wonderful flat-woven floor covering known as a kilim. The term *kilim* is also used for the woven structure employed in these floor coverings and other textiles made by the semi-nomadic weavers—saddlebags and grain bags, tent dividers, pillows, cradles, and tent bands. Kilims were meant to be utilitarian and to add beauty to the family's daily life; they were not considered luxury fabrics. It is only in the twentieth century, with the disappearance of nomadic culture, that these tapestries are receiving the attention and appreciation they deserve from Western collectors.

Owing to the requirements of seasonal work and the patterns of tribal migrations, spinning, dyeing, and even weaving were carried on intermittently. Tools of the trade, from simple drop spindles to looms, were constructed so as to be easily dismantled into components that could be transported by the family's pack animals.

In this culture women made most of the textiles, although men occasionally spun the readily available fleece and hair from their sheep and goats. Weaving skills were an essential accomplishment for a woman and affected her social status. A poor weaver probably could not produce the textiles needed for her own family, whereas an exceptionally good weaver could make more than enough, and the surplus could be sold or bartered.

Only rarely were textile designs recorded on paper or motifs outlined on the warp. Rather, the traditions were passed on within the family from mother to daughter. Each nomadic tribe had a repertoire of design units and color preferences, which daughters learned almost unconsciously while mastering the techniques of fine weaving. The patterns of finished textiles often provided the inspiration for new pieces, but it was not

a common practice to copy another weaving in its entirety.

Colors were produced by dyeing the weft yarn, which consisted mainly of sheep's wool. Historically this involved the gathering, or purchase at local markets, of various plant materials that yielded particular colors. Some of the more familiar ones included indigo (blue), madder root (red), sumac and pomegranate (yellows), and walnuts (brown). The choice of colors depended on tribal preferences as well as the availability of the plants and ease of dye preparation. After processing, the dye material was added to a bath composed of water and substances such as tin or alum that helped make the color permanent.

With few exceptions, slit tapestry was the preferred structure. It could be woven faster than interlocking structures, and its limitations could be compensated for in the design. Kilim patterns rarely incorporate long vertical lines, thus avoiding large, potentially weakening slits in the fabric. Since expendable household items have not been sought by private collectors or public institutions until recently, old examples are scarce. However, a few archaeological fragments and some historical literary references suggest that the slit tapestry structure may have been woven in this part of the world for over twenty-five hundred years.

Because of political and economic changes in the Middle East, the nomadic way of life has almost disappeared. However, many descendants of nomads, who now live in villages and small towns, continue to weave tapestries for urban and foreign markets. They still use natural dyes occasionally, but synthetic colors predominate. The patterns made today are not chosen by the weavers to please themselves; they are created by designers who adapt traditional elements to the tastes of consumers living thousands of miles away. And so, delighted purchasers in Germany, the United States, or Australia provide a market that allows a handweaving tradition to continue a bit longer.

The Urban Tradition

Like many other parts of the world, the Middle East also had an urban textile tradition that included the production of luxury fabrics. In the larger towns, with their extensive trade connections, weavers could choose from a wide variety of fibers, but wool was still favored for tapestry, with silk and metallic threads used to highlight certain pattern elements. In the towns, textile production tended toward specialization. Spinning was done mostly by women, but weaving was primarily a man's profession. Workshops were small, often with only two or three horizontal looms, although some cities in Turkey and Iran had large court workshops that produced fine textiles for the rulers and the elite of society.

In urban areas, tapestry-woven textiles were used mainly for clothing. The Syrian cities of Damascus, Aleppo, and Hama were famous for their abas, many of which had tapestry-work decoration. These simple rectangular garments, open at the center front, served as coats or shoulder mantles. The fabric was a weft-faced, ribbed plain weave, with tapestry-woven ornament inserted during the weaving process so as to appear at the shoulder and center back of the finished garment. The ground fabric was of fine wool or silk, and the tapestry patterning often of silk and metallic threads. From the seventh century on, these abas were prized throughout Syria and Palestine, and owning one was a mark of prestige. Unlike the tapestry tradition of the semi-nomadic tribes, which continues, though in a somewhat altered form, this urban tapestry-weaving tradition virtually disappeared when Syria's textile industry became highly mechanized early in the twentieth century.

In southeastern Iran, in the district of Kerman, many weavers specialized in tapestry work, creating fine, elaborately patterned *shāl* cloth. During the sixteenth and seventeenth centuries this fabric was used as a man's shoulder wrap, and in the nineteenth century it was made into ceremonial

Kilim
Caucasus, 19th century
Wool
Gift of Miss Lily Place   31.81.5

robes for men of the court and worn by upper-class women as a scarf draped around the waist. The weaving was similar to that done in Kashmir, in northern India. Like Kashmiri tapestry, it was a twill structure rather than the more commonly used plain weave. However, since the exceptionally fine fleece used in Kashmir was not available, the Kerman cloth was made of a somewhat coarser, and therefore stronger, wool thread. Nevertheless, it was a spectacular fabric. Many of the pieces that came off the Kerman looms measured somewhat wider and longer than the Kashmiri cloth, perhaps on account of their stronger threads. As with Kashmiri production, during the nineteenth century much of the Kerman *shāl* cloth was made into shawls for export to Europe and America.

Reversible shawl, detail
Kashmir, mid-19th century
Wool
Gift of Mrs. C. C. Bovey   30.62.4

India

India has produced some of the finest tapestry cloth in the world. The tapestry shawl tradition of India began in the sixteenth century, during the Mogul period, and continued into the nineteenth century, when it developed into an industry of great economic importance, with over 450,000 pieces exported in 1861 alone.

In Mogul India the shawl was a wrap used predominantly by men. Finely woven, exceptionally lightweight shawls with tapestry borders were popular at court and were sometimes given by the emperor to nobles as a mark of favor. Through the years, they began to be worn outside court circles, but they always retained an aura of opulence.

In the eighteenth century, European travelers brought Indian shawls home as mementos. First in England and later in France, women adopted them as a fashionable costume accessory. In fact, they became so popular that tapestry-woven copies were made in Scotland, England, and France. But the high production costs of this labor-intensive work made the European shawls more expensive than the Indian imports, and in the early nineteenth century less costly brocaded and printed imitations were introduced as substitutes for tapestry.

Although tapestry shawls were woven in several areas of northern India and in some parts of southeastern Iran, the very finest came from the Indian state of Kashmir. This was due partly to the remarkable skill of the Kashmiri spinners, dyers, and weavers and partly to the availability of the special goat hair needed for the very finest of shawls. The twill tapestry structure with double-interlocked wefts could be woven by many skilled weavers throughout the world, but without the proper fleece, the qualities of light weight and warmth could not be duplicated.

The best fiber came from Tibetan or central Asian goats and sheep, which lived above 14,000 feet. The underfleece that protected the animals from the severe winters of those regions was shed in springtime and gathered by nomadic herdsmen, who sold it in the hill towns to Kashmiri dealers.

Shawl production involved a rather extensive division of labor; twelve or more independent specialists might contribute to the making of one shawl.

Women working in their homes sorted and cleaned the fiber and spun it into yarn. Warp yarn was spun fine and then plied for added strength, whereas the weft remained single but was slightly thicker than the plied warp threads. Finished threads were sent to the dyers.

Weavers' assistants measured the warp thread needed to prepare the loom for weaving. Many shawls required five thousand to eight thousand warp threads, which had to be protected and slightly strengthened with a starch solution before being placed on the loom.

Before the weaving could begin, a pattern had to be made by a pattern-drawer. The drawing was given to a color-caller, who indicated the weft changes needed to weave the design, and these changes were noted on the pattern in a special weaver's shorthand by the pattern-master. On a horizontal loom, the pattern was placed under the warp threads, where it would be visible during the weaving process.

Depending on the width of the cloth, two or three weavers might work at the loom at one time. Individual weft passes, as noted on the design, were called out, and each weaver moved the threads in his area accordingly. Since a double weft interlock was generally used, the cloth line developed evenly across the entire width of the fabric. A large beater built into the loom was used to pack the weft threads in place, instead of the smaller hand-held beaters used with the slit tapestry technique. An ordinary shawl required approximately three months to weave, and an exceptional piece could take up to a year.

In the nineteenth century, when the demand from abroad necessitated increased production, a system of piece weaving was developed: instead of working on an entire shawl, a weaver reproduced one section of the pattern over and over again. This repetition allowed weavers to work faster, and the shorter cloth lengths meant that pieces came off the loom more frequently. The shawl pieces were then sewn together so skillfully that the seams were practically invisible.

Initially workshops were small, but by the mid-nineteenth century some had as many as a hundred looms. Although the work required considerable skill, there was an abundance of

Shawl
Kashmir, mid-19th century
Wool
Gift of Mrs. C. C. Bovey 42.47.9

weavers, and in general they were very poorly paid. Those who profited most were not even the loom owners, but rather the shawl brokers—the middlemen between the producers and foreign merchants. Shawls and the twill tapestry cloth itself were used extensively in India and exported to America, China, Russia, Arabia, the Persian Gulf states, Egypt, and Turkey, as well as to many European countries.

In the 1870s a combination of events—changes in European fashion that virtually eliminated the shawl from the feminine wardrobe, several wars which affected commerce, and famine in India—brought an end to large-scale production of shawls in northern India, including Kashmir. Today a little twill tapestry weaving is still done, but nothing to compare with the masterpieces of the past.

Although the Kashmir shawl is by far the most famous of India's tapestry products, it certainly was not the only Indian woven item with a tapestry structure.

In Bengal, cotton weaving was refined over the centuries to produce cotton fabrics that are unsurpassed. Bengali weavers made exquisite saris with tapestry end panels and side borders. They used the double weft interlock in a plain-weave structure. For the most elaborate decorative patterns, they used metallic threads, which not only gave the garment a more opulent feel, but also added a little extra weight, so the very fine cotton fabric draped more gracefully. These saris were highly valued in India, but they were not exported, and so their production was limited.

In addition to luxury tapestry fabrics, India also produced some domestic tapestry. Most familiar to us is the dhurrie, known today as a flat-woven floor covering but originally designed as bedding. The traditional dhurrie was made of cotton by village weavers for their own use or for sale within the community. It was rarely seen because it was laid directly on a wooden bed frame, with other bedding such as mattresses and sheets on top, completely covering it. In the morning all the bedding was rolled up and put away until evening. In poorer homes dhurries were used as floor coverings, but for the wealthy they served as rug pads and protective undercovers for the more expensive pile carpets.

Traditionally there was little tapestry patterning on dhurries, but toward the end of the nineteenth century the style changed, and the designs on floor coverings and also some of the bedding dhurries became quite elaborate. At this time dhurrie production became a prison industry, and some of the most sophisticated examples were made by the inmates of Indian jails. Slit and common warp tapestry construction were used, as well as the double weft interlock.

Today most bedding is machine made, but with the popularity of flat-woven area rugs, handwoven dhurries are still produced, most of them destined for foreign markets. Traditional techniques continue to be employed, but now a wool weft rather than cotton is often used for floor coverings. As with the flat-woven carpets of the Middle East, the continuance of this weaving seems to be closely connected with the interior design fashions of the West. If these preferences change dramatically, the economic base for production will be gone and in all likelihood an old tradition will cease to be.

China and Japan

Tapestry weaving became popular in China during the later part of the Sung period (960–1279), when it was widely used to copy paintings and calligraphic inscriptions. By the eighteenth century it was employed for almost all textile forms, from interior furnishings and clothing fabrics to special-order altar frontals and temple hangings. The technique was introduced in Japan about 1400, when some priests who had visited China set up their looms at the Ninna-ji temple near Kyoto.

That the tapestry structure was known in the Far East at an earlier date is indicated by Egyptian textiles of the fifth to eighth century found in archaeological excavations in northwestern China and in several Japanese temples. And information has come to light suggesting that tapestry cloth was woven in the Far East much earlier than previously supposed. A small group of Chinese textiles kept for centuries in Tibetan monasteries, and now for sale on the Western art market, appears to substantiate literary references to tapestry production in northwestern China during the Liao dynasty (947–1124). Moreover, research has shown that the famous eighth-century Chinese Buddhist panel known as the Taima Mandala, located in the Taima-dera temple near Nara, Japan, which was long thought to be a painting, is actually a very finely woven silk tapestry with extensive painted restorations.

In both China and Japan, where silk is readily available and widely used for luxury textiles, it is not surprising to find that silk is the fiber most frequently employed in tapestry weaving. It is used for both warp and weft. The warp threads are tightly twisted for strength, whereas the weft threads are loosely twisted so they will pack together easily and cover the warp.

Metallic threads, used in the Middle East since classical times, were not common in China until the Yüan dynasty (1206–1368), when China was part of the vast Mongol empire, with trade connections throughout all of Asia. The metallic threads in Chinese and Japanese tapestries were composed of metal pounded or rolled into an extremely thin sheet. The sheet was attached to a flexible base (often mulberry paper) and cut into

Opposite: *Chair cover*
China, late 17th century
Silk
The John R. Van Derlip Fund   42.8.200

Below: detail

Taoist Immortal, Ho Hsien Ku, detail
China, early 18th century
Silk
The John R. Van Derlip Fund 42.8.339

thin strips, and then each strip was wound around a silk core thread. With a gold alloy, the core thread was often dyed red or yellow to enhance the metallic color.

During the Ch'ing dynasty (1644–1912), the Chinese developed a tapestry style in which the woven image was supplemented with shadings, outlines, and other details painted on after the cloth was removed from the loom. Adding painted details to a tapestry-woven cloth was a practice sometimes employed in other tapestry traditions, but the Chinese used it extensively during the nineteenth century. The painted additions are fairly easy to detect because the change in color does not entirely coincide with the woven structure. Since the color change does not require a new weft thread, there is no corresponding slit at the juncture point.

In both China and Japan, the slit tapestry structure predominated. The fabric was made on a horizontal loom, and the design was almost always woven from bottom to top, that is, as it would be seen in the finished piece. As an aid to the weaver, an outline of the design was sometimes marked on the warp. Because of the light weight and fine weave of the cloth and the rather slick quality of the silk, weavers could pack the weft into place with a lightweight comb or even their fingernails, instead of the heavier beaters used in the Middle East and Europe.

Early Chinese textile production centered on household industry and small-scale workshops with only one or two looms. By the fifteenth century, however, there were merchants who invested their profits in manufacturing, provided the looms, and hired artisans to do the weaving. To keep the manufacturers' costs down, the looms were often located in the weavers' homes. Weavers were supplied with materials and paid when they completed the fabric. Besides such private enterprise, there were the Imperial silkworks in Nanking, Soochow, and Hangchow, which were established in the Ming dynasty (1368–1644) and expanded under the Ch'ing. At the end of the eighteenth century, these workshops had over two thousand looms and almost seven thousand workers.

Like most luxury goods, tapestry cloth was produced mainly in urban centers. There was extensive division of labor, with individual artisans and master weavers specializing in particular design elements. Thus when a team of weavers worked on a hanging or court robe, one might weave all the flowers in the pattern, another would render all the religious symbols, and so on. After filling government and court quotas, weavers could produce textiles for private sale.

Because the technique was so labor-intensive, most tapestry fabric was "woven to shape": only the portion that would show in the finished item was tapestry-woven; the surround area needed for seaming or other unseen uses was a plain, unpatterned fabric. Whether for private individuals or for the court, orders were furnished in fabric lengths. Tailoring and additional adjustments were provided by textile specialists other than weavers.

The Chinese used tapestry for court robes, vests, jackets, costume accessories (insignia panels, rank badges, decorative collars), throne cushions, table and scroll covers, temple banners, altar frontals, and various religious vestments. They also gave these items as ambassadorial gifts, and fine Chinese silk tapestries have influenced the textile traditions of many Far Eastern countries, including Tibet, Bhutan, Nepal, Korea, and Japan.

In Japan, tapestry has been most commonly used for temple hangings, ornamental panels, obis, and curtains for festival carts. Like Chinese fabrics, Japanese tapestry-woven textiles tended to be lightweight and of modest size. Some large pieces in imitation of European wall hangings may have been made in the seventeenth and eighteenth centuries. But tapestries comparable in size to the European ones were not produced in any numbers in the Far East until the late nineteenth century, when Kawashima Mills in Kyota built an unusually large and sturdy loom for the purpose.

Serape, detail
Saltillo area, Mexico, last half of the 19th century
Wool and cotton
Gift of Mrs. Stanley Hawks   78.19.11

The Americas

South America

In pre-Columbian South America textiles were a high art form, and fine cloth, along with silver and slaves, was exacted from conquered peoples as tribute. Although the pre-Columbian weavers did not develop an extensive technology of looms and other mechanical devices, they created complex and diverse woven structures, and textile historians consider them among the finest weavers in the world.

The kingdoms of pre-colonial South America that have been most thoroughly studied were located in what is now Peru and Bolivia. They appear to have been the most advanced cultures on the entire continent. For over five thousand years, empires in the coastal region and later in the Andean highlands rose and fell, and during their periods of dominance, they influenced trade and cultural patterns well beyond the limits of their direct political and military control.

In South America, as in Egypt, ancient textiles have been preserved in desert graves. The west coast of Peru, one of the driest areas in the world, is the source of most of the pre-Columbian textiles so far discovered in South America. The Andean region, on the other hand, has yielded few examples of pre-Columbian weaving; however, many textiles of highland origin have been found on the coast.

Archaeological evidence indicates that by 3000 B.C. cotton was being cultivated on the Peruvian coast, and in the highlands several cameloid animals—alpaca, llama, vicuña—provided hair fibers suitable for weaving. Loom technology developed sometime between 2000 and 1400 B.C., and by 400 B.C. all the textile structures subsequently used in the pre-Columbian period seem to have been established.

In the southern section of the Peruvian coast, in the Paracas region, many textiles dating from the sixth century B.C. have been found that show a high level of technical skill. Local cotton was used extensively, especially for tapestry warp, but camelid yarns were often employed as weft, indicating that even at this early period some trade was carried on between the coast and the highlands. Remains of textiles actually made in the central highlands of Peru or in Tiahuanaco in Bolivia are generally not found in coastal sites earlier than A.D. 500. The sixth-century finds, however, are very impressive, and it is obvious that these inland regions already had a long and rich weaving tradition.

Tapestry appears to have been used primarily for clothing. Slit, warp interlock, single weft interlock, and eccentric weft structures all were used, according to design requirements and cultural preference. Inset tapestry patterning, decorative borders, and separate bands, as well as entire garments, were woven with a tapestry structure.

Until the Spanish conquest in the sixteenth century, the most common weaving materials were the native cotton of the coast and camelid fibers from the highlands. But when the Spaniards introduced sheep to the Americas, the South American tapestry weavers began to use wool also, and later in the century they used some silk, which came to Peru from China by way of Acapulco.

The Spaniards recognized the weaving abilities of the peoples they had conquered. In addition to encouraging the existing production methods, they introduced the horizontal treadle loom, taught men to weave (previously women had been the weavers), and promoted the establishment of small workshops. They also introduced European tapestry styles, and for the next 250 to 300 years the native weavers produced wall hangings, table covers, floor rugs, and ponchos.

In the early nineteenth century the popularity of tapestry weaving declined, and the art has never again been extensively practiced in South America.

Mexico and Guatemala

In Mexico and Guatemala, unlike coastal Peru, burial practices and climate have not favored the preservation of textiles. The earliest textile remains, which are from the state of Chihuahua and La Candelaria cave in northern Mexico, date from about A.D. 1000 to 1600. These fragments and other archaeological evidence point to a fully developed textile tradition and provide some clues to design preferences. But there is not enough evidence to reveal the extent and purposes of the tapestry weaving carried on in this area before the Spanish conquest.

The Spanish influence on Mesoamerican textiles was considerable. As they did in South America, the Spaniards introduced the horizontal treadle loom along with wool and other new fibers such as silk and linen. They taught men to weave and increased production by organizing workshops. By the end of the sixteenth century, a number of Spanish-influenced Indian groups were weaving woolen fabrics.

Navajo "eye-dazzler" blanket
United States, 1890s
Wool
The Christina N. and Swan J. Turnblad Memorial Fund   75.56

As the Spaniards extended their authority in the New World, they had Indians friendly to Spain colonize areas north of Mexico City in an attempt to pacify local populations who persisted in resisting foreign domination. These Indians from the south brought their wool-weaving tradition with them, and by the eighteenth century a regional tapestry style had developed which was used in making the distinctive garments known as Saltillo serapes.

The warp for the Saltillo serape was linen or cotton and the weft was wool, although some later examples contain small amounts of cotton and metallic threads. Most were woven with a slit tapestry structure, but since the design was based on acute angles the slits were so small as to be almost invisible.

The traditional Saltillo serape had three areas of decoration—the outer guard border, the field, and a central geometric figure. At first the central motif was a diamond, but later a scalloped circle was also used. The field and the guard border consisted of small repeated patterns such as lattices, alternating diagonal stripes, or zigzags. Sometimes the fabric was woven on narrow looms, so that two widths with carefully matched patterns would be sewn together to make a single serape.

The town of Saltillo became famous as a place where these serapes were sold in the local market, and the name Saltillo became associated with any finely woven serape of similar design from that region. However, other towns—San Miguel de Allende, Guanajuato, Querétaro, San Luis Potosí, and Zacatecas—are also mentioned in colonial records as producing serapes of comparable quality and design. And many serapes were undoubtedly woven in local hacienda workshops, too.

During the eighteenth and nineteenth centuries, the Saltillo serape was a popular item of male attire, admired beyond the region of northern Mexico where it originated. Weavers as far south as Oaxaca and as far north as the Rio Grande valley in northern New Mexico incorporated Saltillo design elements into their work. But in the twentieth century, as the wearing of national apparel has been abandoned and growing industrialization has created new economic pressures in Mexico, production of the finely woven Saltillo serape has come to an end.

Although the finest tapestry weaving was done in northern Mexico, other areas in Mexico and in highland Guatemala also produced some woolen tapestry blankets. Such pieces are no longer made for a local market, but today Indian weavers make modified versions of these blankets which they sell as wall hangings to tourists. In the Oaxaca region some Zapotec village weavers are working with a few American designers to make tapestry rugs for export to the United States.

In Guatemala, tapestry has never been widely used. Tapestry-woven wool blankets are sometimes carried by men of the Chichicastenango area. The finest Guatemalan tapestries, however, are the beautiful silk hair wraps, or *cintas*, which women wear for religious occasions and holiday celebrations. *Cinta* designs vary from one locality to another. The most elaborate *cintas*, made in several styles and patterns, come from Totonicapán.

The Southwestern United States

In the southwestern United States, fragments of tapestry woven by the Pueblo (Anasazi) Indians have been found which date from A.D. 1100. Remains of narrow bands of plain-weave tapestry and wider fabrics of twill tapestry suggest that the Pueblo employed two weaving methods. Finger manipulation of threads could have been used to make the narrow weavings, whereas loom weaving and the mechanical manipulation of threads would have been required for making the wider, twill tapestries.

Cotton was the preferred fiber, and the slit and single weft interlock were used for inset decoration as well as whole cloth. However, tapestry was never a very popular woven structure with the Pueblo. Rather, it is among the last wave of Indian immigrants to the Southwest that we find people who, once they learned the technique, made it their own and today are the most famous tapestry weavers in North America.

The Navajo arrived in the Southwest sometime after A.D. 1000. They were primarily nomadic raiders and do not appear to have had a strong textile tradition before their close association with the Pueblo in the last decades of the seventeenth century. It was then that Navajo women became acquainted with the vertical loom. During the eighteenth century they mastered weaving techniques and began to develop a distinctive style and gain a reputation as skilled weavers. During this time and well into the nineteenth century, the Saltillo style influenced their weaving, and tapestry patterning with both the slit and the single weft interlock was especially popular among the Navajo.

Before 1865, when they were forced into exile at Bosque Redondo, the Navajo wove primarily to supply their own domestic needs for clothing and blankets. Later, however, they began to produce rugs for an outside market, and Navajo weavers gradually turned from their own design preferences to patterns compatible with the tastes of traders and patrons, mainly Anglo-Americans. By the 1890s their work consisted mostly of rugs for the tourist trade. Regrettable as this may be, the traders and dealers probably saved tapestry weaving in this part of the world from disappearing altogether.

The quality of both technique and design has fluctuated considerably during the twentieth century. Tourism has continued to provide a market for Navajo weaving, and in the past few decades interest in craftsmanship and hand weaving has had a positive effect on quality. Today many Navajo weavers have struck a balance between the aesthetic traditions of their culture and the demands of the marketplace and are producing fine tapestries for wall and floor.

Opposite: *Wise and Foolish Virgins*
Norway, last half of the 17th century
Wool and linen
The William Hood Dunwoody Fund   43.18

Below: detail

Europe

The best-known European tapestry weavings are the magnificent pictorial wall hangings, often called the frescoes of the north. Developed as an opulent form of wall decoration, they also provided insulation against a cold climate and stone architecture, helping to warm the environment both physically and aesthetically.

Fine Egyptian tapestry-woven cloth had been known in Europe since the beginning of the Christian era, but it is difficult to say when the European hangings first appeared in the form familiar to us. The oldest extant tapestries in this style date from the late fourteenth century; however, historical records indicate that large hangings were popular in Europe before then. By the end of the fourteenth century, they were an important element of decoration in the homes of the nobility. Like objects of gold and silver, tapestries constituted a form of portable wealth which gave splendor to the owner's surroundings, whether a castle or a battlefield tent.

Throughout all of Europe, tapestries were a favorite means of displaying wealth and the power and status that wealth implied. Rich nobles formed collections of two or three hundred pieces, and the holdings of royal houses were much larger. Henry VIII had over two thousand tapestries. Often tapestries were made in sets which literally wrapped a room, and they would be changed for special occasions or to suit the owner's whim. In towns and cities, on festival days, tapestries were hung from balconies and on outside walls to contribute to the celebration and to impress the common people. The subjects depicted in these hangings included biblical, mythological, and historical themes, pastoral scenes, courtly pastimes, imaginary scenes of foreign lands, representations of the seasons, and decorative flora and fauna.

These grand wall hangings were designed by some of the most famous artists of the day, and their production entailed very specialized, highly skilled labor. Sheep were bred for the particular qualities of fleece needed for specific types of thread. Spinning, which was done primarily by women in their homes, required considerable proficiency. The fleece had to be properly cleaned and sorted into various wool

Queen Esther and King Ahasuerus
Flanders, mid-15th century
Wool and silk
Gift of Mrs. C. J. Martin for the Charles Jairus Martin Memorial Collection   16.721

grades, and the yarns spun from it had to meet established standards. Warp threads went directly to the weavers' workshops, but the weft was sent to dyehouses to be colored according to the demands of the tapestry design.

The initial rendering of the tapestry design was usually quite small and needed to be enlarged to full size. Sometimes the original artist, but more often trained specialists, working on either paper or canvas, created the "cartoons" which the weavers used as patterns. In the fourteenth and fifteenth centuries tapestry cartoons did not specify every detail, for in that period many artistic decisions concerning individual design elements were left to the weavers. Over time, however, the relationship between tapestry designer and tapestry weaver changed, so that in the eighteenth and nineteenth centuries, the weaver had almost no creative role but slavishly rendered intricate, detailed cartoons.

The many vertical elements in European tapestry designs, and the structural constraints of the weave, made it advantageous to work on the composition from the side rather than building it up from bottom to top. The size of the tapestry, too, determined the direction in which the pattern was woven, and this in turn reflected architectural considerations. Ceiling heights, which were somewhat standard, usually limited the height of hangings to twenty feet or less, but room length and width varied greatly. We know from archival sources that some tapestries were over a hundred feet long. Since a loom was a substantial investment, and the larger it was the more it cost, looms were built to accommodate the smaller dimension of tapestry-woven hangings.

Both horizontal and vertical looms were used for pictorial tapestries in Europe. The horizontal loom had a treadle-operated shedding device, which facilitated faster weaving, but the vertical loom permitted a better view of the fabric while weaving was in progress. Both types allowed several weavers to work side by side on a single tapestry—an advantage in such a time-consuming and labor-intensive craft. The more detailed the design, the longer it took to weave. On many tapestries, a rate of one square yard per weaver per month was usual.

Slit tapestry was the favored structure, and the many openings resulting from this weave were sewn closed after the hanging was removed from the loom. The double weft interlock was employed, too, particularly in borders, where long, uninterrupted vertical lines frequently occurred. Occasionally, other tapestry structures were also used.

Workshops, for the most part, were small, with one to three looms. Some of the larger ones were supported by the state or subsidized by a noble patron. A workshop usually had a master weaver (often the owner in a small shop), who oversaw production. It was he who generally wove the more difficult areas of the design, such as facial features and highly detailed sections, and his name or insignia appeared on the tapestry, often on the guard border. Other weavers might specialize in rendering foliage, architectural elements, and so on. As the weaving progressed, the weavers moved from one area of the tapestry to another, as the design dictated.

Most tapestry weavers were men, but women also followed this trade. Working conditions varied from place to place and also changed over time. Records indicate that in seventeenth-century France boys and girls often began to work between the ages of twelve and fourteen. The young women were paid less and usually quit when their first child was born. Women were generally restricted to work on the vertical loom, because the bent working position required by the horizontal loom was considered unhealthy for them. A number of tapestry workshops were owned by women, usually widows who had inherited the business from their husbands.

The price of tapestries varied considerably. Works commissioned by wealthy aristocrats were very costly, but less expensive pieces, affordable to the aspiring bourgeois, were available from stock.

Nobles often retained a consultant to arrange the details of their tapestry orders. After being apprised of the general requirements of the job—for example, what room the piece would go in and the buyer's preferences of theme and style—the consultant hired an artist to create a suitable image. Then he had the artist or another specialist make a cartoon—an expensive production, especially if the cartoon was painted on canvas. Cartoons could, however, be used again as patterns for other tapestries or hung on the wall as substitutes for the real thing, a practice used to extend the life of the woven hangings, which would be brought out only for feast days and other special occasions. The consultant also chose the workshop that would do the weaving, and at this stage complex negotiations might ensue, for the artist could be an Italian working in Florence and the weavers might be Flemings employed in a Bruges workshop.

Another market was served by workshops that opened retail outlets in major cities. Here a customer could buy a ready-made tapestry or have a piece made to order. Often special orders could be made from modifications of cartoons already owned by the workshop, saving the purchaser a considerable sum. However, some of the pieces sold in these outlets were technically and artistically inferior to the tapestry sets commissioned by the aristocracy.

Most of the finest tapestries were produced in France (Paris, Aubusson, Arras, Beauvais) and Flanders (Tournai, Bruges, Brussels) and exported all over Europe. But the growth of national consciousness, and concern over gold leaving the country in payment for imported luxury goods, led to the establishment of national tapestry workshops subsidized by royal grants. In the sixteenth and seventeenth centuries, Flemish master weavers were hired to develop workshops and train local weavers in Italy, England, Russia, Sweden, Denmark, and Germany. These workshops had their successes, and all produced a number of tapestries in the grand European style. But only in France has a long tapestry tradition remained unbroken. Today the French government still subsidizes the Gobelins, which has been the national workshop since the seventeenth century, and in the town of Aubusson some small workshops continue to produce tapestries.

Besides the grand pictorial hangings, workshops also made other forms of tapestry. These included interior textiles, such as bed hangings, carpets, upholstery fabrics, and pillows, and religious hangings and vestments.

Outside of the commercial workshops, a peasant tapestry-weaving tradition was carried on in some parts of Europe, particularly Scandinavia. This work was done by the women of the household and consisted primarily of domestic goods—pillows; door, table, bench, and bed covers; and small pieces that could be used as wall decoration.

Archaeological remains from the Viking period indicate that tapestry was being woven in Scandinavia in the eighth century. A fragment of a Romanesque-style Norwegian tapestry from the twelfth century suggests that pictorial hangings may have been produced in workshops at that time. In Sweden urban workshops made pictorial hangings beginning in about the sixteenth century and continuing through the eighteenth, but these workshops were attuned to the French styles and appear to have had little influence on the native peasant tradition. In both Norway and Sweden, although a folk pictorial tradition was strong during the eighteenth and nineteenth centuries, the most popular imagery has always been geometric patterning. The weft interlock, both single and double, was generally used, but the common warp interlock was sometimes employed, and slit tapestry was not unknown.

In seventeenth-century Russia, Peter the Great's interest in European culture prompted the establishment of tapestry workshops with the assistance of Flemish weavers. Many fine hangings in the French style were produced in these shops during the seventeenth and eighteenth centuries. In the nineteenth century, a new type of tapestry fabric, used for exceptionally fine floral-patterned shawls, was made by workshops set up on several country estates by landed entrepreneurs. The raw materials were purchased, but every aspect of the manufacture, from fiber cleaning, spinning, and weaving to assembly of the shawl, was performed on the estate, much of it by girls. During the 1830s and 1840s, these workshops turned out award-winning shawls, scarves, and kerchiefs, but production slowed after mid-century and in 1861 the abolition of serfdom shattered the economic base of the workshops.

Courtly Personages in a Landscape
Flanders, early 16th century
Wool and silk
Gift of Mr. and Mrs. James B. Mabon in memory
 of Elsie Smith Mabon   65.9

Each color in a tapestry requires a separate weft. Using the slit technique, a weaver can work on one area of the design at a time, building up the cloth unevenly on the loom. (Diderot, *Encyclopédie*)

Tapestry Techniques

The Woven Structure

A woven structure consists of two sets of threads, the warp and the weft, interlaced on a loom to form cloth. The warp stretches the length of the loom, under tension, and the weft is worked over and under it. In many woven structures the weft threads run back and forth from one edge of the fabric to the other. In tapestry-woven cloth, however, the weft is discontinuous: an individual weft thread is interlaced with the warp only where its particular color is required by the design. Thus the weft threads forming the pattern are essential to the structure of the cloth itself. If they are removed, the whole fabric disintegrates. Generally the tapestry weft entirely covers the warp threads, which do not contribute to the design except as they affect the texture of the cloth.

Other textile techniques, such as brocading, also produce patterned cloth by means of discontinuous wefts. But these discontinuous weft threads are supplementary to a primary weft which runs continuously from one edge of the fabric to the other. The threads forming the design can therefore be removed without destroying the cloth itself. Embroidery is similar in principle, but the supplementary threads that make the pattern are added after the cloth has been removed from the loom.

Slit Tapestry

In the weaving of tapestry cloth, the point where two colors meet is critical. Since each separate area of color consists of an independent weft thread interlaced with the warp, at the juncture of two colors a slit forms in the direction of the warp. If the two colors meet along a diagonal, this is not a serious problem. The wefts progress from one warp to another in the direction of the diagonal, so that only very small slits result and the cloth is fairly stable. Problems do occur, however, with long lines parallel to the warp. They seriously weaken the fabric by causing long slits to form, and for this reason, most tapestry designs contain few long lines in the direction of the warp.

Tapestry makers have always been challenged by the structural limitations of the slit, and they have made of this potential problem a creative design element. European weavers sometimes purposely made a slit within a single area of color, such as a flesh tone, as a means of delineating the nose, eyelids, fingernails, and toes. Coptic, Peruvian, and other ancient weavers also enhanced their tapestry work with slits. And today, too, many tapestry designers find ways to use the slit to advantage.

Cloth made with a continuous weft is woven evenly across the loom, with the exposed, unwoven warp at a right angle to the fabric that has been completed. But with slit tapestry, because the wefts do not go from edge to edge, the cloth can be built up irregularly, with an uneven "cloth line," and the weaver is free to concentrate on one particular area of the design. In addition, the slit technique permits faster weaving because the hands can work continuously, without frequent stops to pick up new weft threads.

The slit tapestry structure has been used all over the world to create colored images in cloth. Weavers in the Middle East, China, Japan, the Americas, and Europe, sometimes using very simple looms, employed this technique to

Slit tapestry

produce clothing, rugs, wall hangings, and other ornamental fabrics, and weavers today use it still.

A slit of any appreciable length, however, does weaken a textile's structure. To overcome the constraints imposed by the slit, weavers devised structural methods of dealing with the juncture of colors in tapestry-woven cloth. The simplest solution—used in many of the large European hangings—was to sew long slits closed after the textile was removed from the loom. The other methods all involve the interlocking of adjacent colored areas so as to eliminate the slit during the weaving process.

Common warp (single dovetail) interlock

Dovetailed interlock

Interlocks

All of the various interlock techniques produce a fairly stable fabric. Using them, however, requires a major change in procedure. The weaver has to maintain a more even cloth line, and the opportunity to concentrate on one facet of the design is lost. The weaver must remain more aware of the overall design as the weaving progresses.

Common Warp

One way of dealing with abutting colors is by wrapping the wefts alternately around the same warp. This gives a line with a somewhat feathered look when viewed closely. The common warp interlock (sometimes called single dovetail) was used by ancient Coptic and Peruvian weavers and is still used today.

A variation of this technique which allows slightly faster weaving and also serves as a design adjunct is the dovetailed interlock. Two or three consecutive passes with weft of one color are alternated with two or three passes with weft of the adjacent color. The resulting line has a notched look. This technique has been used for centuries in several cultures but is probably most popular in Norway and Sweden, appearing in many tapestry-woven cushion covers, coverlets, and wall hangings.

The main disadvantage of eliminating the slit by this method is that thickening occurs along the common warp because it carries twice as many wefts as the adjacent warps, which are covered with only one color.

Interlocking Wefts

Another way to eliminate the slit is the weft interlock, in which adjacent wefts loop around each other on alternate passes. Because the interlock occupies the space between warps, thickening along the join is somewhat less than with the common warp method, and the feathering of the join is less pronounced than with the dovetail. Many examples of this technique can be seen in the clothing, blankets, and rugs made by Navajo weavers in the southwestern United States.

The double weft interlock, a variation of the weft interlock, has been used for centuries by weavers in India, Iran, and Europe. The weaver interlocks the adjacent weft threads on every pass. Although this slows the weaving, the resulting join is very strong, and the join line on the front of the textile is almost as clean as a slit. Thickening along the interlocked wefts is very slight, but a small ridge does form on the surface of the cloth facing the weaver.

Relation of Warp and Weft

It is possible for the tapestry weaver to alter the angle of the warp and weft when working on curvilinear

Single weft interlock

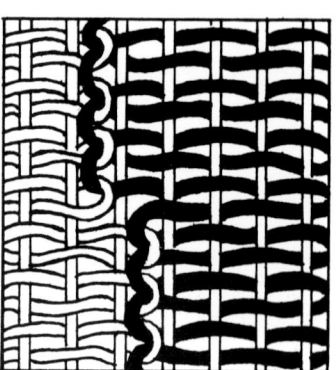

Double weft interlock

forms. This makes for faster production but may also cause surface irregularities such as bubbling on the face of the cloth. Peruvian and Coptic weavers often used this technique, but it is rarely seen in the large European pictorial tapestries. As most of our tapestry terminology comes from the European tradition, a weft of this type is considered distorted and is often referred to as "eccentric."

Some designs are more successful when woven from the side. When finished, this tapestry would have been hung with the warp threads parallel to the floor. The woven image would then be correctly seen as a standing figure leaning over the back of a chair. (Diderot, *Encyclopédie*)

Another means of altering the perpendicular relationship of warp and weft was used in the nineteenth century by the Navajo weavers of the Southwest to create "wedge weave" rugs. Sufficient pressure applied with the weft during the weaving process pulls the warp away from its normal alignment on the loom. If this pressure is maintained during several consecutive weft passes, the warp line in the fabric is permanently displaced. The displacement can be varied within the textile by changing the direction of pressure applied with the weft. Even though the warp in a tapestry is totally covered by the weft, it gives texture to the cloth. Distorting the texture in this manner can enhance the decorative patterning of tapestry-woven rugs and hangings.

Relation of Design and Woven Structure

Although generally hidden by the weft, the warp can play an important role in tapestry design. It gives the fabric a ribbed texture that can be accentuated or diminished according to the number and size of warp threads used. Fairly thick,

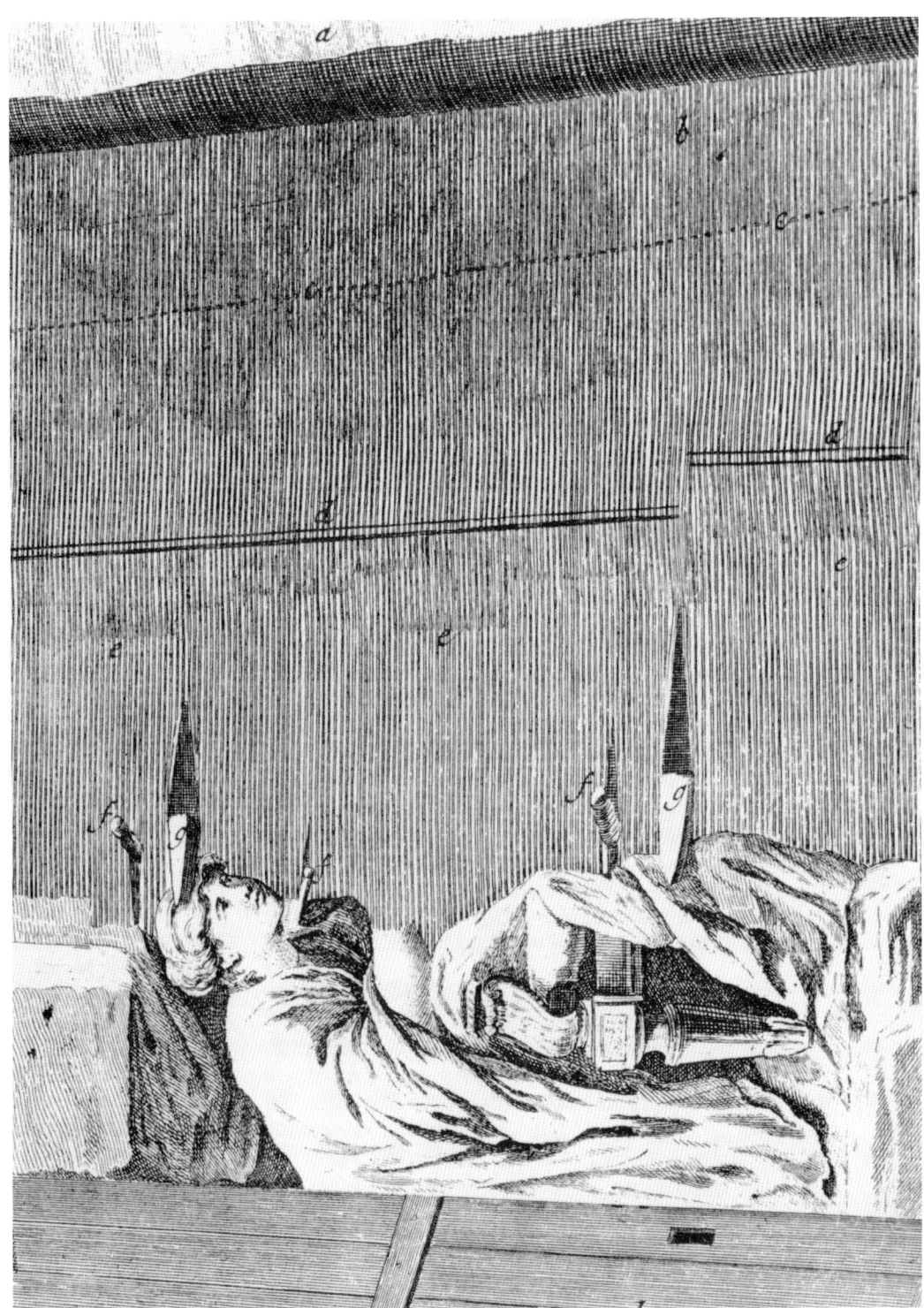

rather widely spaced warps, like those in medieval European pictorial tapestries, produce a strongly ribbed surface, whereas very fine, closely spaced warps, such as those in Kashmir shawls, give a smooth texture.

Whether the warp will be vertical or horizontal with respect to the overall design is determined partly by how the finished cloth is to be used, but beyond that it is largely an aesthetic and technical decision.

To determine how the design can be most effectively woven in relation to the fixed warp, it must be thought of in terms of linear color patterns. A long line of a single color is easier to execute and looks more graceful if it is done with a few long weft passes instead of many short ones. Thus it is more effective artistically, and also more efficient, to weave a linear, Gothic figure when its longest dimension is perpendicular to the warp (giving a horizontal rib) rather than parallel to the warp (giving a vertical rib).

Another consideration is that tapestry weaving is a slow process, and individual design elements will have greater internal continuity if they can be worked on as units. This is made possible by setting up the loom so that the tapestry is woven from the side. The large pictorial tapestries woven in Europe since the fourteenth century are striking examples of this principle. Almost all of these hangings were woven from the side and, when hung, have a horizontal ribbing.

In the twentieth century, the great variety of light sources makes the direction of the rib particularly important, because with tapestry-woven wall hangings, the relationship of the warp rib to the light source can affect the viewer's perception of the design.

Use of Materials

The materials used in weaving tapestries were at first limited to locally available fibers. But as trade routes expanded, a greater variety of weaving materials could be obtained, especially by producers of luxury goods, whose clients could afford the very finest.

For centuries textile makers have experimented with various fibers to develop threads with structural and aesthetic characteristics that enhance the luxury fabrics they produce. The warp and the weft have different functions and therefore require different types of threads.

Warp

Generally the warp threads must be stronger than the weft, for they are under considerable tension on the loom and frequently assume the weight-bearing stress in the finished cloth. Since fibers become stronger as they are twisted together, warp threads are more tightly spun than weft threads. As more fibers are added the thread becomes thicker, and this also contributes to its strength.

The surface of the warp must be smooth enough to allow the weft to pack down and fully delineate the pattern. But with some fabrics, a warp that is too smooth can also present problems: movement and gravity may cause the weft to continue packing down after the cloth has been removed from the loom. Such rearrangement of the weft can result in distortion of the pattern.

Since a tapestry warp is almost always completely covered, how it looks is of little concern. To maintain structural consistency, however, only one type of thread is used for warp in any given weaving. Usually the fiber for the warp is selected from readily available material and spun to specific requirements.

For centuries wool was the most commonly used warp fiber in Europe. In the early nineteenth century, with the mechanization of cotton thread production, cotton became a favorite. Flax (used for linen thread) was almost always employed by ancient Egyptian weavers, and this fiber has long been popular with Scandinavian weavers. In the Far East, silk has always been preferred.

Weft

Except in the Far East, wool is by far the most popular weft fiber. Its elasticity and loft make a thread which expands to give good warp coverage. And wool also absorbs dyes well, an important quality in a tapestry weft.

For special effects, other kinds of fibers can be introduced into the weft. Coptic weavers and also many European tapestry weavers often used silk threads. In the Middle East, when white was needed in the design, cotton was occasionally employed. Weavers of various cultures have enriched their textiles with gold, silver, and other metallic threads.

An eighteenth-century tapestry workshop, France. Several weavers are at work on one tapestry. (Diderot, *Encyclopédie*)

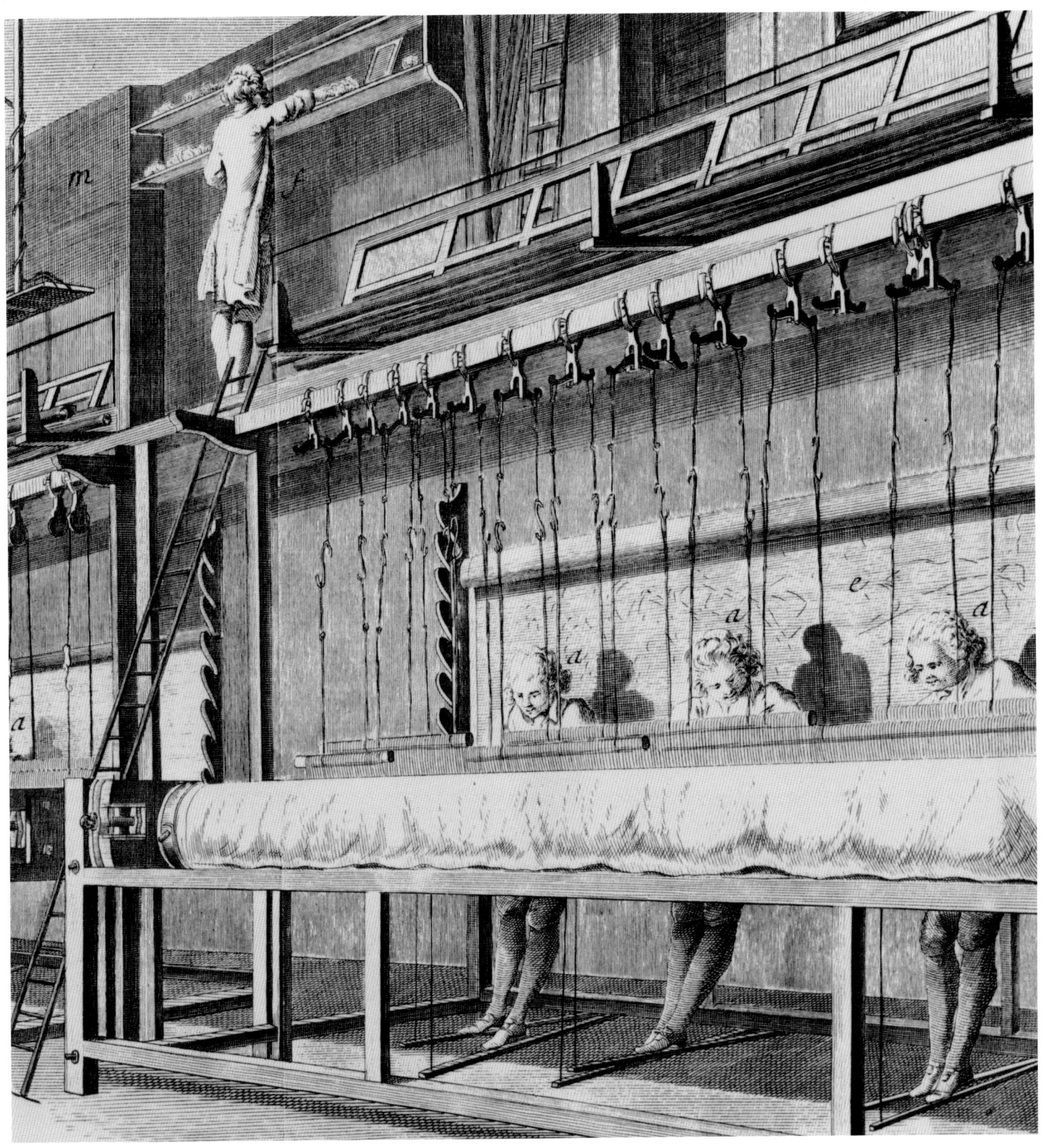

Appendix: Tapestry-Woven Textiles in The Minneapolis Institute of Arts

Tapestries were among the first textiles collected by The Minneapolis Institute of Arts. In 1915 Mrs. C. J. Martin, working with director Joseph Breck, purchased for the museum the first of several large European hangings that form the Charles Jairus Martin Memorial Collection. Three other women with a lifelong love of textiles also contributed to the development of the museum's tapestry holdings. Miss Lily Place gave a number of Middle Eastern rugs and garments that she had acquired in the 1920s, while living in Egypt. During the 1930s and 1940s, the Institute received Kashmir shawls and Navajo blankets and rugs collected by Mrs. C. C. Bovey. And in 1978 Mrs. Stanley Hawks, the wife of a diplomat who served in Guatemala and Mexico during the 1920s, gave the museum her textile collection, which included a number of tapestry-woven pieces.

Egypt
The museum owns nine woven Egyptian textiles, five of which have tapestry patterning. All five date from the fourth to the seventh century, and two are large pieces with figural decoration.

The Middle East
There are 13 tapestry-woven pieces made in the Middle East: 10 kilims (one Caucasian, 4 Persian, and 5 Turkish), 2 Syrian abas, and one Turkish hand towel. Most of them came to the museum in the 1920s and were probably made during the nineteenth century. Some of the "Kashmir" shawls that are currently listed as Indian may actually have been woven in southeastern Iran, and careful research is needed to ascertain their origins. There are also two coats, classified as nineteenth-century Persian, in which tapestry-woven fabric forms part of the appliqué design. At present, the museum is not actively collecting Middle Eastern textiles, but there are several small private holdings in the community and at least one active collector.

India
The Institute owns 35 Kashmir shawls and a number of twill tapestry shawl fragments. These represent a full range of styles, from the long, minimally patterned pieces of the early nineteenth century to the elaborately patterned square shawls of the mid-nineteenth century. Four of the shawls are reversible. In addition to the twill-woven tapestry pieces, the collection contains one cotton dhurrie and, from the Bengal area, four cotton saris with tapestry end panels.

China and Japan
Most of the approximately 150 silk tapestry pieces from the Far East are Chinese. Six were made in the seventeenth century and 66 in the eighteenth. The rest were woven in the nineteenth century. The collection consists primarily of costume pieces but also includes altar frontals, banners, chair and cushion covers, and some hangings. These pieces are under the jurisdiction of the Department of Asian Art.

The Americas
Of the 60 examples of tapestry from the Americas, 17 are pre-Columbian fragments woven in coastal Peru and the Andean highlands. There are 11 Mexican pieces, 5 of which are in the Saltillo style. The other pieces were made in the southwestern United States, most of them between 1890 and 1920. A major local private collection contains a number of fine chief blankets as well as "eye dazzlers" and other Navajo pieces.

Europe
The Institute's collection of European wall hangings is internationally known for its high quality and historical importance. Especially noteworthy are the early Flemish hangings and several fine pieces from the famous "Artemisia" set woven in the seventeenth century for the French royal family. Of the 46 European tapestry pieces in the collection, most of them wall hangings, 22 are Flemish (3 from the fifteenth century, 14 from the sixteenth, and 5 from the seventeenth) and 16 are French (one from the sixteenth century, 10 from the seventeenth, 4 from the eighteenth, and one from the nineteenth). Two of the French hangings were designed by François Boucher; the nineteenth-century piece is an Aubusson carpet. Three pieces come from Italy, and one each from Holland, Sweden, and Norway. And there are two Russian ecclesiastical vestments—a silk maniple and matching stole—from the late nineteenth or early twentieth century. As funds permit and as pieces are available, the museum will continue to acquire exceptionally fine European tapestry, particularly in areas not now represented in the collection.